T0149327

Dr. Yvonne Lee-Wilson

THE RISE & FALL OF WOMEN IN MINISTRY

The Journal

No weapon that is formed against thee shall prosper; and every tongue that shall rise against thee in judgment thou shalt condemn. This is the heritage of the servants of the LORD, and their righteousness is of me, saith the LORD.

Isaiah 54:17

authorHOUSE®

AuthorHouse™
1663 Liberty Drive
Bloomington, IN 47403
www.authorhouse.com
Phone: 1 (800) 839-8640

Published by AuthorHouse 03/23/2016

ISBN: 978-1-5049-8542-0 (sc)
ISBN: 978-1-5049-8540-6 (hc)
ISBN: 978-1-5049-8541-3 (e)

Library of Congress Control Number: 2016904305

Print information available on the last page.

Any people depicted in stock imagery provided by Thinkstock are models, and such images are being used for illustrative purposes only. Certain stock imagery © Thinkstock.

This book is printed on acid-free paper.

Jesus served...
as the

Original, diligent and faithful servant.
<u>*His*</u>

Undying will to *seek and to save that which was lost...*

Required the attributes of One, *Whose* countenance exhibited uncompromising obedience, love and humility.

Now is the time!
This temporal world needs a committed and compassionate people, who know they have been called and chosen to pick up the mantle of our Lord and Savior, Jesus Christ...

And live in example, for *all* to witness, in the effort that souls may be saved. As a result, Believers in Christ will fervently...

Live unto the glory of the Lord, as their *stories* will empower others to possess the desire to exhibit the countenance that is continually pleasing to the Lord, for **He created us for eternity!**

Table of Contents

My God...

Without You, I am nothing!
In You, I live and move and have my being (Acts-
17:28). Your grace and mercy have brought me
through the trenches of life. As a believer, suffering
is a privilege, for it is a test of our faith!
Though trials have come...
I will not murmur and complain, but I rejoice, with Joy!
With You, I am able to express my inner feelings
and beliefs. I can tell my story and not be
ashamed, for Our Relationship is grounded in
love, and my faith is girded in Your Promises.
Thank You Lord, for not giving up on me!

**In all this you greatly rejoice, though
now for a little while you may have had
to suffer grief in all kinds of trials.
These have come so that the proven genuineness
of your faith of greater worth than gold,
which perishes even though refined by fire
may result in praise, glory and honor
when Jesus Christ is revealed.
(1 Peter 1:6-7)**

Your Servant,
Apostle Yvonne Lee-Wilson

This journal is dedicated in memory of:

Dr. Yvonne Baylock,
avid educator, chaplain and intercessor,
who served as an instrumental advocate
of upholding essential family values.
Dr. Baylock, my mentor and friend, deemed it
necessary to remain stedfast upon truth,
according to the doctrine of Jesus Christ.
She wore many hats, but most important, she
diligently served, as God's faithful servant, who
coined the words, "If it isn't written, it isn't said."
Well, *this* is the product of the written, and
I fervently say to the people:
Let's continue to STAND on the Promises of
God, in spite of the face of adversity,
opposition, discrimination and persecution.

You have been called and chosen to RISE...
solely in God's Appointed Time.

Since the book,
THE RISE AND FALL OF WOMEN IN MINISRTY,
was released in 2008, God has moved mightily!

My Family is *still* standing in harmony
and solidarity, through
fortification of God's love, grace and mercy.

My mother, Elder Louise Lee-Snipes,
Thank you for never leaving my side.

My new stepfather, Charles Snipes,
Thank you for living this holy life.

My aunt, Reverend Evy Johnson,
Keep praising Him,
for I have kept the faith, in the midst of all my storms!

My brother, Minister Reginald Lee, who went to be with the Lord, will always be remembered as a man whose exemplary character caused anything contrary, to the will of God, to *cease and desist!*

Elder Kenneth T. Lee, my biological brother
and integral leader in the body of Christ,
Thank you for holding me accountable,
according to the Word of
God. You are a man of great wisdom, with a profound
message to educate, encourage and inspire others,
through the teachings of Christ. You are the one, who
has charged me to preach to the masses, and with
you standing and walking beside me in Ministry, I
continue to remain grounded, by grace and humility.

Ray, Carl, and Travis,
I am blessed to have *real* men of God, as my brothers.

My brother, Bishop Anthony Lee,
Thank you for being a strong tower in the ministry.
Many souls have been saved, through your teachings
of the Word, *for* you exemplify the meaning of
preaching the unadulterated doctrine of Jesus
Christ. I never could have made it, without you!

My younger sister, Elder Geneva Davis,
you have inspired many lives, with your *Dorcas spirit;*
continue to aide the wounded and neglected.

My youngest sister, Evelene Lee-Cole
and brother-in-law, Johnny Cole,
Thank you for standing in the gap for my great
grandchildren: Kynnedi, Kamora, Kaelyn, and Jacoby.
They will lead lives that are grounded in truth,
due to consistent impartation of your wise counseling.

The Lord blessed me with three daughters!
Words alone, cannot express my love for you:
Shantina Lee,
Thank you for your commitment to the *Ministry*
of Helps. You have evolved into a woman of
great wisdom, who will not hesitate
to reach out and help those, who are less fortunate.

Prophet Taneshia Lee,
Thank you for promoting the legacy of the
Real Women of God Fellowship and submitting to the
authority, God has established within me. I respect
and honor you, as a woman of Godly character,
emitting much wisdom, integrity, and humility.
Continue to serve in the Office of the Prophet,
as God has ordained for you.

Tarina Yvonne (*In Glory, 2003*)
my youngest daughter, with a big heart...
Many people were touched by her pleasant demeanor
and warm smile. Tarina was not afraid to *be herself,*
while in the presence of others, and as a personal
mandate, I have become *transparent,* before the people.

Praise the Lord!
for My grandchildren are college-bound:
Evelene, Amber, Brittany, Brianna, Phillip, and Justin.
Jaleel, I will always love you.

The Lord called my spiritual father, Bishop Arthur
M. Cofield, home to Glory, and I miss him greatly!
The man of God left the mantle for me to carry...
I can hear him *now...*
"It's marvelous, in His eyes!"

Kelly Gandy, my spiritual daughter,
You never stopped teaching the children, and I
thank you, *for* keeping THE RISE AND FALL OF
WOMEN IN MINISTRY, *The Journal, alive!*

To my spiritual mother, Chief Apostle Joanna Bean
and my pastor, who led me to this
work, Evangelist Rose Jones,
I am eternally grateful for the spiritual guidance
that I have received from both of you.

July 2, 2014, a day I will always remember...
That was the day, the enemy attacked
my husband, Adelbert
Wilson, but God saw fit to keep him
in the Land of the Living.
Since that day, he has made remarkable recovery and
continues to praise the Lord for His grace and mercy!

You see, my story never stops being
told, so keep telling yours;
pen the words you feel, but cannot say.
I made a vow to The Lord, and I can't take it back!

I must write...
I am so grateful for all that God is
doing in my life, as well as
others', who respect the God in me and trust
that the anointing is real. I am speaking of the
people, who do not dishonor the work that He has
given me, to advance the Kingdom of God.

It's my story, and it's not personal...
for I owe it all to *my God!*

As you file through the pages of this journal,
I pray that you reach a *spiritual climax,* the
turning point of knowing...*Why* YOU have not
given up or given in, conformed to the ways of
this world, or not bound by worries and fears.
Here's your reminder...
Without faith it is impossible to please God for anyone
who comes to Him must believe that He exists and
that He rewards those who earnestly seek Him.
(Hebrews 11:6)

To the diligent servant in the body of Christ:
I DARE YOU!
to take inventory of *Self*

I CHALLENGE YOU!
to search the depths of the surface and discover
what is lying dormant within your soul

I CHARGE YOU!
to **Examine yourselves to see whether**
you are in the faith; test
yourselves. Do you not realize that
Christ Jesus is in you—
unless, of course, you fail the test? (2 Corinthians 13:5)
~ Kelly Gandy, Editor

YOU ARE HERE!

THE POINT OF NO RETURN...
Your heart may be heavy, and words cannot
express the pain. You know too much to turn back,
but the road ahead seems dim... Where are all
my friends, who promised to be by my side?
Where are all the souls, to whom I have ministered?
You realize that you are standing alone.
You've reached a crossroad...
You do not know which way to turn, but...
**Look unto Jesus, the author and finisher of our faith;
who for the joy that was set before him endured
the cross, despising the shame, and is set down
at the right hand of the throne of God. (Hebrews 12:2)**

EXPERIENCE YOUR AWAKENING... Just
when you think you have lost your *Voice,* Now
is the time to journal; pen your story... *Here
I am, Lord, right where you want me.
I surrender! I will obey!
Use me... for Your Glory!*

Throughout this journey, you will be reminded that we are tested and tried *but* not forsaken. You will acknowledge and accept that *brokenness* is not a bad *state,* for it is *the place,* where you have made a conscious decision to **stand fast therefore in the liberty wherewith Christ hath made us free, and be not entangled *again* with the yoke of bondage. (Galatians 5:1)**

~ Apostle Yvonne Lee-Wilson, PhD.

We are troubled on every side, yet not distressed;
we are perplexed, but not in despair; persecuted,
but not forsaken; cast down, but not
destroyed. (2 Corinthians 4:8 and 9)

Chapter I
MY STORY, MY GOD

"The enemy had set a trap for me. He scheduled a permanent fall, but did not know this was the open door to the Kingdom."

1. Read the chapter, in its entirety.

2. Define the term, "fall," from a natural and spiritual perspective.
Is there any correlation between the two? *Explain.*

3. **Biblical Review:** Find an individual in the Bible, who experienced a Great Fall. Parallel the character's story to your personal journey.
Include Scripture.

4. **Personal Reflection:** Pen your story.

**I am in a great strait: let me fall now into the hand of the LORD; for very great are his mercies: but let me not fall into the hand of man.
1 Chronicles 21:13**

Define the term, "fall," from a natural
and spiritual perspective.
Is there any correlation between the two? *Explain.*

_____

_____

_____

_____

_____

_____

_____

_____

_____

_____

_____

_____

Faith is to believe what you do not see;
the reward of this faith is to see what you believe.
~ Saint Augustine ~

_____

_____

_____

_____

_____

_____

_____

_____

_____

_____

_____

_____

Seeds of faith are always within us;
sometimes it takes a crisis to nourish
and encourage their growth.
~ Susan L. Taylor ~

Biblical Review: Find a character in the Bible, who experienced a Great Fall. Parallel the character's story to your personal journey.

_____

_____

_____

_____

_____

_____

_____

_____

_____

_____

_____

_____

_____

Faith is taking the first step
even when you don't see the whole staircase.
~ Dr. Martin Luther King, Jr. ~

Every tomorrow has two handles. We can take hold of
it with the handle of anxiety or the handle of faith.
~ Henry Ward Beecher ~

Pen Your Story.

_____

_____

_____

_____

_____

_____

_____

_____

_____

_____

_____

_____

_____

Problems are not stop signs, they are guidelines.
~ Robert H. Schuller ~

7

_____

_____

_____

_____

_____

_____

_____

_____

_____

_____

_____

_____

_____

_____

_____

Faith and prayer are the vitamins of the soul;
man cannot live in health without them.
~ Mahalia Jackson ~

_____

_____

_____

_____

_____

_____

_____

_____

_____

_____

_____

_____

_____

Faith is different from proof;
the latter is human, the former is a Gift from God.
~ Blaise Pascal ~

Chapter II
BROKEN AND STILL WHOLE

"Jesus goes beyond the pain; the disappointment and anger, the lies, shame and guilt, betrayal, and most of all... fear."

1. Read the chapter, in its entirety.

2. Is there a literal and spiritual connection of being *broken and yet whole?* Explain. *Include Scripture, to support your response.*

"Through our struggles and tormented circumstances, such as, mental, physical, and emotional abuse, the loss of a loved one, and the encounter of spiritual warfare, we are broken in the natural and spiritual realms, and Jesus is the only Potter, able to mend us.
When I am totally healed, delivered, and made whole, (Jeremiah 18:6; Isaiah 64:8) then, I'll RISE, YET, THIS IS ONLY THE BEGINNING..."
-An Excerpt, The Rise and Fall of Women in Ministry

3. Personal Reflection: *This is only the beginning...*

**The sacrifices of God are a broken spirit:
a broken and a contrite heart, O
God, you will not despise.
Psalm 51:17**

Is there a literal and spiritual connection of being *broken and yet whole?* Explain. *Include Scripture, to support your response.*

_____

_____

_____

_____

_____

_____

_____

_____

_____

_____

_____

_____

God is always in control and He will never leave us.
~ Allyson Felix ~

_____

_____

_____

_____

_____

_____

_____

_____

_____

_____

_____

_____

*What gives me the most hope every day is
God's grace; knowing that his grace is going
to give me the strength for whatever I face,
knowing that nothing is a surprise to God.*
~ Rick Warren ~

This is only the beginning...

_____

_____

_____

_____

_____

_____

_____

_____

_____

_____

_____

_____

*In my deepest, darkest moments, what really got me
through was a prayer. Sometimes my prayer was
"Help me." Sometimes my prayer was "Thank you."
~ Iyanla Vanzant ~*

14

_____

_____

_____

_____

_____

_____

_____

_____

_____

_____

_____

_____

_____

*Darkness comes. In the middle of it, the future looks
blank. The temptation to quit is huge. Don't. You are in
good company... You will argue with yourself that there
is no way forward, but with God, nothing is impossible.*
~ John Piper ~

Cast your cares on God; that anchor holds.
~ Frank Moore Crosby ~

Chapter III
IT'S NOT PERSONAL

"I can certainly say that it's not personal, when my body was "racked" in pain, as I lay, on my bed of affliction, for it wasn't about me. It was about the souls to whom I would minister, *in* a lost and dying world."

1. Read the chapter, in its entirety.

2. *"The higher you are elevated, the more targets fired to destroy you..."* Do you agree or disagree? *Please explain.*

3. How can *taking things personal* hinder us from continually seeking the Kingdom of God?

4. **Personal Reflection:** *It's not personal when...*

There hath no temptation taken you but such as is common to man: but God is faithful, who will not suffer you to be tempted above that ye are able; but will with the temptation also make a way to escape, that ye may be able to bear it. 1 Corinthians 10:13

"The higher you are elevated, the more targets fired to destroy you..." Do you agree or disagree? *Please explain.*

_____

_____

_____

_____

_____

_____

_____

_____

_____

_____

_____

_____

_____

Knowledge of God's Word is a bulwark against deception, temptation, accusation, even persecution.
~ Edwin Louis Cole ~

_God will not permit any troubles to come upon
us, unless He has a specific plan by which great
blessing can come out of the difficulty._
~ Peter Marshall ~

How can *taking things personal* hinder us from
continually seeking the Kingdom of God?

_____

_____

_____

_____

_____

_____

_____

_____

_____

_____

_____

_____

*Our heavenly Father understands our disappointment,
suffering, pain, fear, and doubt. He is always there
to encourage our hearts and help us understand
that He's sufficient for all of our needs.*
~ Charles Stanley ~

_____

_____

_____

_____

_____

_____

_____

_____

_____

_____

_____

_____

_____

_____

_____

The most important lesson that I have learned
is to trust God in every circumstance.
~ Allyson Felix ~

It's not personal when...

_____

_____

_____

_____

_____

_____

_____

_____

_____

_____

_____

_____

As we advance in life it becomes more and more
difficult, but in fighting the difficulties,
the inmost strength of the heart is developed.
~ Vincent Van Gogh ~

22

_____

_____

_____

_____

_____

_____

_____

_____

_____

_____

_____

_____

_____

_____

It doesn't take a lot of strength to hang on.
It takes a lot of strength to let go.
~ J. C. Watts ~

God's mercy is fresh and new every morning.
~ Joyce Meyer ~

Chapter IV
CHOSEN AND SOMETIMES FORGOTTEN

**"How can someone not want to accept the
fact that they have been forgotten, by the
world, and yet, chosen by God?"**

1. Read the chapter, in its entirety.

2. Do you ever feel "chosen" *and sometimes* forgotten?

3. Does the introductory scripture to the
chapter have any significant impact on being
***chosen and* sometimes forgotten?**

4. Can the terms, *called* and *chosen*
be used interchangeably,
or do they each hold respective meanings and must
be carefully and properly used in context?

5. **Personal Reflection:** *I've been chosen and...*

***Many are called but few are chosen
Matthew 22:14***

Do you ever feel "chosen" *and sometimes* forgotten?

_____

_____

_____

_____

_____

_____

_____

_____

_____

_____

_____

_____

Where there is no struggle, there is no strength.
~ Oprah Winfrey ~

It is during our darkest moments that
we must focus to see the light.
~ Aristotle Onassis ~

Does the introductory scripture, to the
chapter, have any significant impact on being
chosen <u>*and*</u> *sometimes forgotten?*

_____

_____

_____

_____

_____

_____

_____

_____

_____

_____

_____

*It is your passion that empowers you to do
that thing you were created to do.*
~ T.D. Jakes ~

_____

_____

_____

_____

_____

_____

_____

_____

_____

_____

_____

_____

_____

_____

You may not control all the events that happen to
you, but you can decide not to be reduced by them.
~ Maya Angelou ~

Can the terms, *called* and *chosen* be used
interchangeably, *or* do they each hold respective meanings
and must be carefully and properly used in context?

_____

_____

_____

_____

_____

_____

_____

_____

_____

*Holding on to anger, resentment and hurt
only gives you tense muscles, a headache and
a sore jaw from clenching your teeth.
Forgiveness gives you back the laughter
and the lightness in your life.*
~ Joan Lunden ~

_____

_____

_____

_____

_____

_____

_____

_____

_____

_____

_____

_____

_____

_____

Remember, the storm is a good opportunity for the pine and the cypress to show their strength and their stability.
~ Ho Chi Minh ~

I've been chosen and...

_____

_____

_____

_____

_____

_____

_____

_____

_____

_____

_____

*The God we serve does not seek out the perfect,
but instead uses our imperfections and our
shortcomings for His greater good. I am humbled
by my own limitations. But where I am weak,
He is strong.
~ Rick Perry ~*

Great works are performed not by
strength, but perseverance.
~ Samuel Jackson ~

_____

_____

_____

_____

_____

_____

_____

_____

_____

_____

_____

_____

_____

_____

What is to give light must endure burning.
~ Viktor E. Frankl ~

Chapter V
WHEN WOMEN RISE

"When women rise...to support one another, encourage, inspire, and empower one another, and speak into the lives of others, then we can invite change; however, change can only come when we expect to receive it!"

1. Read the chapter, in its entirety.

2. **Biblical Review:** Find a woman in the Bible to whom you mostly relate; compare/contrast the charge on her life to diligently and boldly do the work of the Lord to the mantle *which* He has placed on your life. *Include Scripture.*

3. **Personal Reflection:** When women RISE...

For unto whomsoever much is given, of him shall be much required: and to whom men have committed much, *of* him they will ask the more.
Luke 12:48

Biblical Review: Find a woman in the Bible
to whom you mostly relate; compare/contrast
the charge on her life to diligently and boldly
do the work of the Lord to the mantle
which He has placed on your life.

_____

_____

_____

_____

_____

_____

_____

_____

_____

_____

Permanence, perseverance and persistence in spite of
all obstacle(s), discouragement(s), and impossibilities:
That distinguishes the strong soul from the weak.
~ Thomas Carlyle ~

_____

_____

_____

_____

_____

_____

_____

_____

_____

_____

_____

_____

_____

_____

Character cannot be developed in ease and quiet. Only through experience of trial and suffering can the soul be strengthened, ambition inspired, and success achieved.
~ Helen Keller ~

When women RISE...

_____

_____

_____

_____

_____

_____

_____

_____

_____

_____

_____

_____

_____

There is more power in unity than division.
~ Emanuel Cleaver ~

_____

_____

_____

_____

_____

_____

_____

_____

_____

_____

_____

_____

We gain strength, and courage, and
confidence by each experience in which we
really stop to look fear in the face...
we must do that which we think we cannot.
~ Eleanor Roosevelt ~

Where there is unity there is always victory.
~ Publilius Syrus ~

Chapter VI
IS IT GOD OR THE ENEMY?

**"Is God the Author of your story? Is He the
One, Who chose you? Did God heal you?
Is He the One, Who saved you? Is
God the One, Who blessed you? Is He the One,
Who raised you from your fall? Is God the
One, Who has authority in your life? Then,
why are we giving *place* to the enemy?"**

1. Read the chapter, in its entirety.

2. *When we fall, it is not always bad.
It is for the benefit of the
Kingdom, so that when we rise, we
may bless the body of Christ.*
Do you agree or disagree? Please explain.

3. *Is there scripture that supports your response?*

4. **Personal Reflection:** *When a door
is shut, God opens a window.
He always makes a way for you to
escape the trap of the enemy.
Share your testimony.
Include scripture, to support your response.*

The thief cometh not, but for to steal, and to kill, and to destroy: I am come that they might have life, and that they might have it more abundantly.

John 10:10

When we fall, it is not always bad. It is for the benefit of the Kingdom, so that when we rise, we may bless the body of Christ. Do you agree or disagree? Please explain. *Is there scripture that supports your response?*

_____

_____

_____

_____

_____

_____

_____

_____

_____

_____

_____

_____

_____

Strength and growth come only through
continuous effort and struggle.
~ Napoleon Hill ~

_____

_____

_____

_____

_____

_____

_____

_____

_____

_____

_____

_____

_____

Find a place inside where there's joy,
and the joy will burn out the pain.
~ Joseph Campbell ~

Share your testimony.

_____

_____

_____

_____

_____

_____

_____

_____

_____

_____

_____

_____

_____

Faith activates God - Fear activates the Enemy
~ Joel Osteen ~

_____

_____

_____

_____

_____

_____

_____

_____

_____

_____

_____

_____

_____

Some of God's greatest gifts are unanswered prayers.
~ Garth Brooks ~

_____

_____

_____

_____

_____

_____

_____

_____

_____

_____

_____

He who has faith has an inward reservoir of
courage, hope, confidence, calmness, and
assuring trust that all will come out well
- even though to the world it may
appear to come out most badly.
~ B. C. Forbes ~

Chapter VII
WHAT A GREAT FALL

"My pride fell. My pain fell. My heart fell. My spirit-man fell. My mind-set fell. The mind–set, of which I am speaking, hindered me from recognizing the destined mission that God scheduled for my life."

1. Read the chapter, in its entirety.

2. *We do not understand the height of the dimension of God's elevation for us, until we have fallen...*
Can you identify with this statement? Does it speak volumes to you? Please share...

3. *If God does not give me the green light to GO! I'm not moving. I'm in a good place!*
Please state what this proclamation means to you.

4. **Personal Reflection:** *"Lord, I'm going to serve You, with all my..."*

And we know that all things work together for good to them that love God, to them who are <u>the called</u> according to his purpose
Romans 8:28

48

*We do not understand the height of the dimension
of God's elevation for us, until we have fallen...*
Can you identify with this statement? Does
it speak volumes to you? Please share...

_____

_____

_____

_____

_____

_____

_____

_____

_____

_____

_____

*Strength does not come from winning. Your struggles
develop your strengths. When you go through hardships
and decide not to surrender, that is strength.*
~ Arnold Schwarzenegger ~

We are twice armed if we fight with faith.
~ Plato ~

If God does not give me the green light to GO!
I'm not moving. I'm in a good place!
Please state what this proclamation means to you.

_____

_____

_____

_____

_____

_____

_____

_____

_____

_____

_____

The patriot who feels himself in the service of
God, who acknowledges Him in all his ways,
has the promise of Almighty direction, and will
find His Word in his greatest darkness.
~ Francis Scott Key ~

51

A hero is an ordinary individual who finds the strength to persevere and endure in spite of overwhelming obstacles.
~ Christopher Reeve ~

"Lord, I'm going to serve You, with all my..."

_____

_____

_____

_____

_____

_____

_____

_____

_____

_____

_____

_____

*There are many things that are essential to arriving
at true peace of mind; one of the most important is
faith, which cannot be acquired without prayer.*
~ John Wooden ~

_Out of suffering have emerged the strongest souls;
the most massive characters are seared with scars._
~ Khalil Gibran ~

_____

_____

_____

_____

_____

_____

_____

_____

_____

_____

_____

_____

_____

_____

Love your enemies, bless them that curse you,
do good to them that hate you, and pray for them which
despitefully use you, and persecute you (Matthew 5:44).
~ Jesus Christ ~

The End

yet this is just the beginning...

Index of Scripture

- 1 Chronicles 21:13
- Psalms 51:17, 147:3
- Proverbs 3:5-6, 27:17
- Isaiah 26:3, 53:4-5, 54:17, 61:1
- Matthew 5:10, 44, 9:37, 16:19, 22:14, 25:21
- Luke 4:18,12:48
- John 1:12-13, 10:10, 14:12, 15:13
- Romans 8:28
- 1 Corinthians 9:22, 10:13, 13:7-8, 15:58
- 2 Corinthians 4:8-9, 13:5
- Galatians 5:1
- Ephesians 6:10-18
- Philippians 2:5, 10-11, 4:6
- Colossians 3:23-24
- 1 Thessalonians 5:17
- Hebrews 11:1-6, 12:2
- James 5:16
- 1 Peter 1:6-9, 4:10-11

Spending time with God through prayer and His Word
is a prerequisite for having a great life
and fulfilling your purpose.
~ Joyce Meyer ~

A Special Thank You

To those who have encouraged me in my quest
to journal and advance the Kingdom of God:

Apostle Carol and Dr. Duane Sherman
Prophet Provedencia Blanchard-
Harris & Brother Roy Harris

Therefore, my beloved brethren, be ye stedfast,
unmoveable, always abounding in the work
of the Lord, forasmuch as ye know that
your labour is not in vain in the Lord.
(1 Corinthians 15:58)

Alderman Carrie Austin
Lady Dianne Turner Roseland Manor All
Saints Residents Margaret Woodside

Thank you for your words of encouragement
and expression of kindness. I praise God
for your loyalty to Ministry!

My Pastor, Brenda Brown, you live by example,
according to the doctrine of Jesus Christ, and
I honor you for your exemplary disposition.

My devoted congregation, *Body of Christ Deliverance Ministries,* You have remained faithful in service to the body of Christ. Without faithful followers, who are willing to intercede and labor on my behalf, I could not effectively do *This Work.*

Minister Tracie Richardson, the word, *Abba,* is an Aramaic term that is closely translated as *Daddy.* I often hear you giving honor to our "Daddy, God," in reverence to the unique and intimate relationship that we share with our Heavenly Father. As we proclaim, God is our *Abba Father!* We are His children, all who are born-again, according to John 1:12-13.

Minister LaTonja Golden and Minister Carol Coleman, Body of Christ Youth Ministry is grasping the real meaning of being a servant, unto the Lord. Through your teachings of Christ, the youth are beginning to display love and humility towards one another, as well as others. Continue to teach our children the Word of the Lord.

Minister Elaine Presberry, the psalmist, continue to minister to the people, as we render the petition, *Walk With Me, Lord, While I'm On This Tedious Journey...*

Minister Sheila Love and Minister Leslie Williams,
Your labor of love has been a heart-
felt experience to *all*... Please,
continue to extend kindness and
generosity to God's people.

Minister Lolita Luckett, Many are hurting,
from abuse, abandonment, rejection... If
we return to our first love, Jesus
Christ, we will experience *Real Love,*
through our Lord and Savior.
**Greater love hath no man than this, that a
man lay down his life for his friends.
(John 15:13)**

Minister Dorothy Borders,
Thank you for holding me accountable, according to the
Word of God.
The Bible says, Iron sharpeneth iron; so a man sharpeneth
the countenance of his friend. **(Proverbs 27:17)**

Pastor Brenda Yvonne Smith of
Changed Lives Prayer Ministry,
birthing out an anointed Ministry is a powerful process!
It requires total submission and obedience unto the Lord.
You must be sensitive to the voice of God
and allow the Holy Spirit to guide you into all
truth (John 16:13). As God's chosen vessel, you
have remained diligent in fasting and praying,
while spreading the Gospel of Jesus Christ.
There have been enduring times, as well as triumphs!
While *man* opposes, God approves!
When faced with adversity, your faith increased!
Where there is Vision, there is *pro*vision.
Where there is purpose, there is promise,
for when God has a plan for your life,
it may take time to manifest,
but it will come to past… in HIS appointed time.

Mother Brantley, Pastor Rochelle Brantley,
Ronald, Reginald, Raymond, Becandice, Cauis,
Elvie, Lawanda, Andrew, Amanda, Aunt Rita,
and the families, connected to Dr. Yvonne
Baylock, the mother, daughter, sister, wife...
Prayer Warrior, Mother of the Roseland Hospital
Staff, Chaplain, Nurse, and so much more...
There will never be anyone like her.

To the family,
Thank you for sharing Dr. Baylock
with me, for over 15 years.
To God be the Glory!

"I am a pillar of *Body of Christ Deliverance Ministries;*
this is where I will transition, if The
Lord doesn't say different."
~ *Dr. Yvonne Baylock*

My Godmother, Evangelist Doris Lee,
you have birthed and raised greatness!

**Isaiah 53:4-5 reads: Surely he hath borne our griefs,
and carried our sorrows: yet we did esteem him
stricken, smitten of God, and afflicted. But he was
wounded for our transgressions, he was bruised for
our iniquities: the chastisement of our peace was
upon him; and with his stripes we are healed.**

My *Godmother*, Sylvia Moore, *God daughter*,
Tierra Rose, and *God sisters*, Leslie and Robyn,
without sincere love and commitment to one
another, where would we *be* today?
It is an honor to have you in my life, *always...*

*My Godmother, Josephine Wade, Owner of Captain's
Hard Times,* you are the epitome of demonstrating
quality service, with a warm smile. You have
served God's people well, and for that reason alone,
you have witnessed the Lord's increase...

Dr. Sandra Cobham,
You were the one, who embedded in
my spirit, "Lord I thank you."
In spite of our afflictions and infirmities...
In the midst of the most tumultuous
storm, Praise the Lord!

I pray that the Lord will bless these souls and use them in the Kingdom, evermore...

*Apostle Denise Clark Apostle Edith
Wright Apostle Virgil Jones
Apostle Sylvester Brinson, III
Apostle Beverly London
Apostle Robbie C. & Apostle Sharon Peters
Apostle Derrick Shephard*

**The Spirit of the Lord GOD is upon
me; because the LORD
hath anointed me to preach good
tidings unto the meek;
he hath sent me to bind up the brokenhearted, to
proclaim liberty to the captives, and the opening of
the prison to them that are bound. (Isaiah 61:1)**

*Apostle Elsie Bridges
Apostle Glendora Harris
Apostle Timothy & Pastor Dorothy Peoples
Apostle Shaunette Houghton
Bishop John & Kindra Rodgers
Bishop Linda C. Shearrill
Pastor Napoleon & Evangelist Bettye Hollister*

**Verily, verily, I say unto you, He that believeth on me,
the works that I do shall he do also; and greater works
than these shall he do; because I go unto my Father.
(John 14:12)**

The *greater works* are in progress...

Pastor Constance T. Crawford

Well done, good and faithful servant! You have been faithful with a few things; I will put you in charge of many things. (Matthew 25:21)

Evangelist Carolyn Wilson
Evangelist Debra Brooks
Evangelist Wanda Walker
Joyce Chapman

To the weak I became weak, that I might win the weak. I have become all things to all people, that by all means I might save some. (1 Corinthians 9:22)

Pastor Patricia Hymon-Kidd
Pastor Larry & Dr. Faye Rogers
Pastor James Austin
Pastor Shirley Richardson
Reverend Barbara Dudley
Dr. Joann Coleman

Jesus said to His disciples, "The harvest truly is plenteous, but the labourers are few." (Matthew 9:37)

Let us continue to be among the faithful and compassionate laborers of *His Harvest,* so that souls may be saved and used for the Kingdom.

Gidget Moore-Hopper
Angela Scott
Coach Clara Debrie
Elisha Wilson
Catholic Charities Transitional Coaches

**Whatever you do, work at it with all your
heart, as working for the Lord, not for human
masters, since you know that you will receive
an inheritance from the Lord as a reward.
It is the Lord Christ you are serving.
(Colossians 3:23-24)**

Pastor Olivia Paige
Pastor Ivy Scott-Jones
Pastor Octavia and Pastor Mark Morgan
Pastor Larry and Pastor Barbara Jefferson
Dr. Harriet P. Jamison
Dr. Jamesa Humphrey

**Blessed are they which are persecuted
for righteousness' sake:
for theirs is the kingdom of heaven. (Matthew 5:10)**

You exhibit the true representation of Christ.

Evangelist Cora
Chaplain Marie

We need soldiers, engaging in warfare, to pray on behalf of others, according to **Ephesians 6:18,** which tells us to *keep praying* for all of God's people.

*Evangelist Tonya
Harris Evangelist Rosa Shaw
Minister Roslyn Smith
Evangelist Sharon Rolark
Pastor Ella Scott, the woman who
really knows my story...
The Daughters of Zion and Angela*

The Bible says, **Pray without ceasing.
(1 Thessalonians 5:17)**

Thank you for your prayers and labor of
love towards my family and me.

Evangelist Bessie,
Keep shouting His name, Jesus!

The Bible says, **At the name of Jesus every knee
should bow, of things in heaven, and things in
earth, and things under the earth; And that
every tongue should confess that Jesus Christ
is Lord, to the glory of God the Father.
(Philippians 2:10-11)**

Minister Izetta Gray
Minister Veroncia Bracey
Phillip Snowden
Bishop and Yolanda Pate (Kalamazoo Michigan)
Apostle Jack and Evangelist Doris Carter Apostle
Eunita Reynolds

**As every man hath received the gift, even so
minister the same one to another, as good
stewards of the manifold grace of God. If any
man speak, let him speak as the oracles of God;
if any man minister, let him do it as of the ability
which God giveth: that God in all things may
be glorified through Jesus Christ, to whom be
praise and dominion for ever and ever. Amen.
(1 Peter 4:10-11)**

Continue to use your *gifts* to glorify our Heavenly Father.

The Purity Sisters:
Pastor Barbara Weathersby
Pastor Rochelle Brantley
Minister Tracie Richardson
Evangelist Bessie Williams
Evangelist Tonya Harris
Chaplain Marie Parker-McKenzie
Mother Zodie Richardson
Sister Denise Williams
Brenda Evans
Diane Ard

**I beseech you therefore, brethren, by the mercies of God, that ye present your bodies a living sacrifice, holy, acceptable unto God, which is your reasonable service.
And be not conformed to this world: but be ye transformed by the renewing of your mind, that ye may prove what is that good, and acceptable, and perfect, will of God.
(Romans 12:1-2)**

Anita Stewart-Montgomery,
a wonderful woman of God, you always
reminded me of how much I encouraged
your walk with God and Ministry
Reverend Russell Montgomery,
Thank you for being a faithful servant!
Always remember the promise of **Jeremiah 29:11.**
To God be the Glory!

**There are many more, who have not been listed,
but I am still writing...**

In Him and through Him, in the unity of the Holy
Spirit, we receive strength and courage, to STAND
boldly, with our faith girded in truth! Come what may,
God won't turn His Back, or have respect of persons.

**Great is His Faithfulness; His Mercies
begin afresh each day
(Lamentations 3:23).**

.

I say to myself,
"The Lord is my inheritance; therefore,
I can beareth all things,
believeth all things, and endureth all things,
according to the Word of God"(Refer
to 1 Corinthians 13:7 and 8).

Apostle Yvonne Lee-Wilson, *PhD.*
Senior Pastor
Body of Christ Deliverance Ministries

Dr. Yvonne Lee-Wilson, *PhD* is a Board-Certified Life Coach with AACC, Chaplain, and orator, serving within the Five-Fold Ministry, as well as Spiritual Intercessor for Alderman Carrie Austin, *Ward 34 of Chicago.*

For speaking engagements or other Ministry Service, contact: (312) 882-3180 *or* info@bodyofchristdelmin.com.
P.O. Box 288813
Chicago, Il 60628

Printed in the United States
By Bookmasters